THE URBAN MARKET
Magazine

MAY 2022

2022 Teen Writer's Cohort
Advocacy Through Writing

Halee Simons
Philip Wiggins
Moriah Finley
Beloved Joshua Simons
Majesty Finley

The Latest On
Ukraine
More Healing or Further Hurt?

Education, Leadership, Urban Youth,
Business Strategies
Resources For The Urban Market

DTDYouth X Edition
September 24, 2022

ITS TIME TO GO DEEP SUMMIT
September 22 - 24, 2022

EDITOR'S LETTER

I believe in providing a solution to the problems in my community, family, and industries while leaving a legacy in the interim. One day our existence will diminish in the wind, but the impact will continue onward and upward. In this edition of The Urban Market Magazine, you will find solutions to concerns in urban communities. We continue to change the narrative from what was to what is.

The world is an exciting place to be in right now. We have made it past the pandemics, and the world we knew has shifted to new variances. With this shift comes new opportunities to take a deeper dive and impact through knowledge, education, awareness, and action.

My vision is to strengthen the pathway for urban youth to the untapped possibilities of the world while providing resources to the urban market through systemic support. My greatest hope remains to reduce disparities plaguing urban families while bridging the demonstrating the need for a much-needed active pathway between youth and business opportunities.

The urban market is centered around the urban community, and the heart of the urban community remains urban families. Urban families, urban communities, and the urban market are filled with opportunities to elevate self and businesses.
I am an award-winning and best-selling author of many books that focus on leadership, urban youth, urban communities, the urban market, education, and the triathlon sport. I have written the books and the curriculum during and beyond my doctoral process, stemming from my 2006 leadership and education models (non-secular and secular).

I have been seen on Fox45, WBAL, and WJZ, in the Baltimore Sun, in international publications such as USA Triathlon Magazine, and media with the United States Olympic and Paralympic Movement, to name a few.

My vision for this publication is to educate and bring awareness to urban communities' concerns and introduce viable solutions to do business in the urban market. This publication will do just that in addition to work that falls under DTD Enterprises, LLC's purview. Under DTD Enterprises, LLC umbrella includes DTD's Urban Multisport Consulting Firm, DTD Urban TV Network, DTD School of Urban Leadership, The Urban Market Magazine, DTD's Urban Multisport Radio/Podcast Show, DTD Academy for Urban Youth, The International Association of Black Triathletes, The IABT Junior Multisport Club, and IABT Multisport Racing.

I have spoken locally and globally while hosting conferences/events to showcase positive transformational change. Will it ever be enough? One will never know, so until then, the advocacy, leadership, vision, and innovation continues.
I have worked and impacted young minds through K-12, undergrad, and graduate programs spanning over three decades plus. One of my signature programs is DTD Sports Academy 4 Urban Youth. DTD Sports Academy 4 Urban Youth transforms urban youth into exceptional leaders through changed behavior, advocacy, civic engagement, and buy-in. One of the subprograms includes my 2022 Teen Writer's Cohort, which assists urban youth in lending their voice to change through the mighty pen. Learn more www.urbanmultisportconsulting.com

A Dive Deep Academy is another signature program designed for individuals who desire to do or expand their business to the urban market. A Deep Dive Academy provides personal development and business development training that assists in launching or scaling a business or building community relationships. Learn more www.adeepdiveacademy.com

Check out their articles and remain inspired, encouraged, motivated, and on fire. The greatest gift we can provide to the current and next generations is opportunities. Opportunities to be seen and heard while developing their skillsets to take their proper placement in their future endeavors.
Learn more about programs, services, books, and curricula at www.urbanmultisportconsulting.com.

CONTENTS

SECTION 1

04	*Diversity, Equity, Inclusion & Access (Urban Community)*
08	*Leadership vs Managing Transformational Change*
11	*Concerns with Business In The US*
14	*Unemployment and Underemployment In Urban Communities*
17	*Urban Communities & Transportation Concerns*
19	*Lack of Preparation Programs For Youth*
22	*The Plight of Education In Urban Districts*
25	*Doing Business In The Urban Market*
28	*Leadership Training and Development Through Continuous Education Opportunities*
29	*Urban Youth & Education*
32	*Advocacy & Leadership (Urban Youth*

SECTION II

35	SPECIAL ISSUE: UKRAINE

SECTION III
TEEN WRITER'S COHORT (FLIER)

39	*School Should Have More Fun*
42	*Finances Leadership & Education*
48	*TEENPRENEURS U.N.I.T.E. To Build Your Own Wealth*
50	*Finances, Education, and College & Career Readiness*
55	*School Protection*

LACK OF PREPARATION PROGRAMS FOR YOUTH

DOING BUSINESS IN THE URBAN MARKET

DIVERSITY, EQUITY, INCLUSION, AND ACCESS BEACH

(URBAN COMMUNITY)

By Yana Rybak

The modern city is a densely populated area, much more than before. Life in the city is quite complex. Every day people face new challenges related to the differences between the social groups that occupy the city.

On the other hand, various social groups face daily challenges in adapting urban society and the city's infrastructure to the needs of vulnerable groups.

The city must create an atmosphere where diversity, equity, inclusion, and access play a key role in solving this problem.

Diversity.

It tells us that there are different groups of people and recognizes them. Defining characteristics can be:

- nationality, race, religion
- sex
- sexual orientation
- age
- language
- mental and physical abilities
- family status
- political views.

Research has shown, for example, that men more than women with equal qualifications and skills are favored in employment. We must solve such a problem in a developed society. We must also promote the employment of individuals with disabilities.

What does equity mean?

The main objective of equity is to ensure similar opportunities for all, and to eliminate barriers that prevent anyone from dealing with urban issues and participating in public processes. It also includes fairness, impartiality, and honesty towards each one and every person by public or private institutions and society.

Inclusion

It can be defined as how each team member feels involved and valued. It supports a warm environment, allowing everyone to feel like an active participant in the urban community. It aims to reduce unconscious and conscious biases. A person should not feel excluded because of his characteristics.

Access.

That means using the benefits of civilization regardless of belonging to any social group. The absence of barriers will allow full participation in the city's economic, political, and social life. Sometimes the differences between inclusion and access are blurred. These are continuous processes for estimating existing barriers. Society must be creative and use its coping skills to overcome such blocks.

Why are Diversity, Equity, Inclusion and Access important?

These concepts are practical for building a comfortable, equal, and happy urban community. The vital issue is prevention and combating discrimination.

A city that lives by these principles should put them into practice, for example, in urban development programs, employment policies, etc.

Following urban developments should be designed, planned, and built on the principles of access and inclusion.

Unfortunately, the transport system remains a big problem for people with disabilities, especially those who use power wheelchairs. Many of the transport services, such as carsharing, are also unavailable.

Public open spaces, parking lots, crosswalks, transport, and bus stops should be accessible to people with disabilities. Elements of the road environment should consider the need for movement of individuals with disabilities. Public and private institutions should provide access for these individuals too. Social and educational structures must be changed to allow the development of all kinds of citizens.

The risk of isolating such people is too high, and the urban community should increase such people's involvement in urban processes.

Everyone should have honest and equal opportunities to enjoy urban services without discrimination and harassment.

Holistic Health and Wellness LLC provides a wide range of comprehensive personalized solutions to address your individual needs. We provide evidence-based treatment for mental illness and substance use disorders. We offer a variety of services ranging from medication management to genetic testing to provide individuals with an effective client centered treatment plan. In helping you achieve optimal physical and mental health; a dedicated team of qualified professionals will work with you to design a treatment plan that meets your needs.

All of our services are provided in a calm, nurturing, and non-judgmental environment where the clients get complete privacy and confidentiality. Our aim is to not just provide mental health and medication services, but we also assist individuals in enhancing their capacity towards successful living, recapturing their integrated role in the community and society.

Battling mental illness can be extremely difficult for both the patients and their families. People experiencing a mental health condition, such as depression and bipolar are at a higher risk for suicide than the general population. Mental illness can have an impact on the overall well-being of a person, including their physical health. There are a number of medical conditions that have been linked to mental health disorders, such as heart condition, hypertension, cancer, and stroke. Here at Holistic Health and Wellness LLC we use the latest research and innovative data to provide evidence-based treatment for you or your loved ones, who may be dealing with mental health or substance use disorders.

We accept most major health insurance plan, for most services. Give us a call today to see if your plan is accepted!

LEADERSHIP VS MANAGING TRANSFORMATIONAL CHANGE

BY YANA RYBAK

At first glance, these two notions seem to be very similar, if not identical. However, their meaning is suddenly very different.

The purpose of any change is usually to increase the productivity and utility of the workforce.

It is necessary to consider its role and impact in achieving the goal of understanding the difference between leadership and managing transformational change.

MANAGING TRANSFORMATIONAL CHANGE.

Transformational changes are aimed at a complete change of business processes. They are usually cardinal, so they can cause resistance among staff.

There are several examples of such changes in the organization of the company:

- reform or replacement of the offered products and services;
- introduction of new technologies;
- significant strategic changes.

There are several stages of human adaptation to change:

- Shock. Characterized by denial and non-acceptance of new changes. Can be displayed in a radically negative attitude to what is happening.
- Anger. The second stage. It is embodied in active protests against the introduction of changes. An individual may feel the need to adapt and not want to. He may also think that his existing position may be shaken.
- Acceptance. The person finishes thinking about the negative consequences of changes and begins to implement them, study, and investigate.
- Commitment. The change goal can be reached at this stage when the person fully applies the new modifications, and his work becomes effective.
- Some skills are needed to manage transformational change to ensure that people are not stuck in the first two stages for a long time.

What are they?

We can determine several characteristics of effective management of transformational change:

- planning the introduction of new methods in advance;
- honest information about innovations and their objectives;
- the constant support of the reasons for changes;
- ongoing monitoring of change implementation;
- the ability to minimize stress and unfavorable effects of innovation.

So management is a process of continual performance monitoring. It aims to keep staff engagement and support.

HOW IS LEADERSHIP FUNDAMENTALLY DIFFERENT?

Leadership inspires trust in the leader, pride, and self-esteem. That leads to natural internal processes of understanding the importance of change.

The actions of a leader, in this case, are aimed at shaping positive changes in people with the idea of transforming them from followers to leaders. They will not only be able to adapt to the changes but also promote them. Leadership is more closely linked to the idea, the initiation of change, ensuring speed of implementation, efficiency, and effectiveness.

This concept is broader and deeper than managing transformational change and has the following characteristics:

- Influence. It is not about physical force or violence but about authority, which motivates us to do more than is required;
- Activity. Rapid decision-making, acceptance of risk, and use of innovative techniques.

A leader allows others to act, motivates, and inspires. It distinguishes leadership from the technical management of transformational change. Leadership has a more effective impact on implementing change in such a case.

TAKING THE ORDINARY TO EXTRAORDINARY!

918-900-2019

www.xtraconsulting.com

FEATURED SERVICES

ED TRAINING MODULES
- Executive Director Training Modules
- Executive Director/CEO Coaching and Consulting

GRANT WRITING
- Grant Prospect Research
- Grant Readiness Consultation

BUSINESS PLANNING

CUSTOMER SERVICE TRAINING

PROGRAM ASSESSMENT & EVALUATION
- Program Data Collection & Analysis
- Program Innovation and Redesign
- Program Outcomes and Measurements

SPEAKING ENGAGEMENTS
- Sponsor A Podcast

SMALL BUSINESS MARKETING
- Social Media Management (Lite)
- Website Redesign

BOARD TRAINING AND DEVELOPMENT

FUNDRAISING PLAN
- Fundraising Strategizing Sessions
- Fundraising Development and Consulting
- Event Planning Consultation

DIETARY ASSESSMENT AND CONSULTATION

RESTAURANT ASSESSMENT AND CONSULTATION

STRATEGIC PLANNING

CUSTOMIZED BUSINESS AND **PROFESSIONAL SERVICES AVAILABLE**

CONCERNS WITH BUSINESS IN THE US

BY OYEYEMIAYO W.

The United States of America remains one of the top countries to start a business in the 21st century, owning to the country's reliable and consistent economy and its constant development. According to the world bank, the U.S. ranks 55th as one of the countries where it is easy to start a business. Many business owners want to invest and operate locally in the U.S., and this is increasingly improving the country's economy. Like in every other country, specific policies and rules have been implemented regarding how every business should be overseen. Aspects like taxes, trading across borders, and technology are becoming concerns for business owners and citizens. Some of these concerns have been curated.

Taxes

Businesses in the U.S. are expected to pay tax depending on the revenue, size, type of operation, and other rules guiding the company's location. The U.S. has undergone significant tax and economic changes, split into the federal, state, and local levels. The country is focusing mainly on protecting its industries and maximizing its tax receipts; hence there have been recent tax changes to regulate international trade. According to reports, the U.S.'s corporate tax rate is projected to rise to 28.00 percent in 2022, a significant increase from 21.00 percent, which it was in 2020-2021.

The forecast of other tax rates for 2022 includes:

- The Sales tax rate is projected to rise by 0.00 percent.
- The personal income tax rate at 37.00 percent.
- The social security tax rate is still at 6.2% for the employer and 6.2% for the employee.

Trading

Canada and Mexico are the two major border trade partners in the U.S. However, Canada remains the top trading partner in terms of U.S. export sales. The U.S. has always been an attractive market for foreign countries, although it is estimated that China will have larger companies than the United States and Europe in the next decade. Markets are worldwide and more competitive now than ever before. Also, the US-Mexico-Canada (USMCA) agreement which replaced the North American Free Trade Agreement (NAFTA), ensures labor and environmental rights are protected and favors the interest of the farming and automotive industries.

Technology

Due to new technological discoveries, businesses can now scale faster with ease while using little capital. More businesses are investing in technology, which can be felt in the level of their customer satisfaction. Thus, it is becoming easier for startups to grow and compete with large, established businesses. This new development has also improved efficiency in the decision-making process.

In essence, business in the United States is continually evolving, as with other countries. The economy is ever-changing with intense competition in the global market. Company owners cannot overemphasize the importance of building quality contact and networking. Having an educated workforce and investing in important technology will help improve individual businesses. Also, proper tax planning will help companies effectively use their financial resources.

PEER TUTORS OF MARYLAND

MATH AND READING
GROUP AND 1-1 SESSIONS

SCHOOL YEAR PROGRAM

SCHEDULE

FREE STUDY HALL 4:00-4:30 PM
(TUES/THURSDAY)

MATH GROUPS - TUESDAY & THURSDAY
1ST - 7TH GRADE GROUPS   4:30-5:30 PM
8TH - 12TH GRADE GROUPS   5:30-6:30 PM
DROP IN TIME   6:30-7:30 PM

READING GROUPS - TUESDAY & THURSDAY
8TH - 12TH GRADE GROUPS   4:30-5:30 PM
1ST - 7TH GRADE GROUPS   5:30-6:30 PM

CREATIVE WRITING - WEDNESDAY
3RD - 12TH GRADE GROUPS   5:30-6:30 PM

1-1 SESSIONS - TUES/WED/THURS
1ST - 12TH GRADE   4:30-8:30 PM
READING AND/OR MATH

PRICING (TOTAL FOR SESSION)

GROUP STUDY
ONCE/WEEK 1-1 (PEER TUTOR) $125
TWICE/WEEK 1-1 (PEER TUTOR) $225
ONCE/WEEK 1-1 (TEACHER) $425
TWICE/WEEK 1-1 (TEACHER) $500
                                   $1000

*ALL GROUP STUDY IS RUN BY A PTM TEACHER
*SIBLING DISCOUNT OF $25 PER CHILD

HOW TO SIGN UP

REGISTER NOW AT
PEERTUTORSOFMARYLAND.COM
AND LET'S ACE IT TOGETHER!

CONTACT MR. FIELD
E: FIELDJUS@GMAIL.COM
P: (586) 484-4828

UNEMPLOYMENT AND UNDEREMPLOYMENT IN URBAN COMMUNITIES

BY OYEYEMIAYO W.

Unemployment and underemployment are becoming salient issues worldwide, and American urban communities are not left out of this development with an increase in the number of job seekers and underpaid workers. Some Americans find it hard to get sustainable jobs, and even those employed are forced to work in low-paying and low-skill jobs despite their qualifications.

A common phenomenon In urban areas is educated unemployment. Many youths with graduate and postgraduate degrees are not able to find jobs. The coronavirus crisis led to an increase in the unemployment rate soaring to 14.7% in the U.S. The economic recession and cycling of businesses also play a role in the increased unemployment rate.

However, the rate of unemployment in the U.S seems to have declined recently, as, in March 2022, it was recorded by the U.S. Bureau of Labor Statistics (BLS) to be 3.6%. Still, there are many job seekers, especially in urban communities. This unemployment and underemployment rate has affected many individuals, making it difficult to sustain themselves. It also causes psychological, financial, and emotional stress on the unemployed and low-income earners in the long term. Individuals are happier when they can be productive and valuable to society and family by paying bills and meeting needs. Without the ability to do this, illness and depression can set in. Some causes of unemployment and underemployment In urban areas are

Mass migration

Mass migration is a significant cause of unemployment in urban areas. Many people are leaving the rural communities to seek jobs in urban areas, leading to overcrowding. Whenever there is any unfavorable condition or drought, people migrate from rural areas in large groups, increasing the population of the urban city. Unfortunately, the city may not be well prepared to cater to their needs and provide employment opportunities for all immigrants, leading to mass unemployment.

Technological change

Improved technology has also caused a decrease in employment because job opportunities that staff members carried out have been replaced by technology to make it faster and easier. For instance, some companies have replaced jobs meant for cashiers and cafeteria workers with vending machines.

Labor demand deficiency

Labor demand deficiency is also referred to as cyclical unemployment. Labor demand deficiency occurs when there are more applicants than jobs available. Low consumer demand creates cyclical unemployment. When there is no sale, companies lose too much profit, leading to a decline in demand. If this decline continues and sales do not pick up immediately, they begin to lay off workers to maximize profit. It is cyclical because the increase in unemployment causes consumer demand to drop, even more, leading to large-scale unemployment.

Consequently, the employment rate in a country determines the strength of its economy, which shows the level of satisfaction or dissatisfaction of citizens with its government and leaders. Hence, unemployment and underemployment in urban communities are significant issues that should be addressed without delay.

The Adamant Agency

Building Unshakeable Lives and Businesses From the Inside Out

We're a business and leadership development consulting and education firm helping you transform your business with smart strategies, better leaders and cohesive teams, and the right systems that ensure your business runs like a fine-tuned machine, even when you're on vacation.

Be a Strong CEO & Leader

Define your company's vision, design the strategic plan, and lead your team to achieve it. AND have more time to work **ON** your business, not just **IN** it, and learn to lead from your values.

Right Systems & Teams

Systems are **KEY** to business success and freedom. Having the right systems in place allows you to attract the right team for your business culture and provides the foundation they need to produce great results.

Book A Consultation Today

 757.560.1768

www.theadamantagency.com   info@theadamantagency.com

By Oyeyemiayo W.

URBAN COMMUNITIES AND TRANSPORTATION CONCERNS

Urban communities are the dream place for everyone because of the beautiful ambiance and refined infrastructures, making it easier to carry out daily activities. However, as appealing as these features are, they also come with some disadvantages. One of such is the increased population these cities have to accommodate, leading to a crowded environment as commuters are constantly trying to get to work or school simultaneously. Discomforts such as traffic and finding suitable parking spaces set in, making transportation a significant concern for urban communities. We have curated some transportation concerns in urban communities.

Traffic congestion

Traffic congestion is a result of an inadequate system of movement. Traffic congestion often occurs when transportation in an urban community can no longer accommodate the level of movement it used to. There are several causes of traffic congestion: construction, collisions, overloading, and road debris. The number of public transportation, private cars, and commercial vehicles is increasing daily without the development of urban roads. However, the state of traffic in different urban communities varies. According to the INRIX scorecard, while American Urban cities like Boston, MA, experience an average of 164 hours in traffic annually, Philadelphia, PA spends only 112 hours, and Los Angeles, CA spends about 138 hours annually. INRIX Scorecard denotes the geographic location of facilities that can curb traffic conversations.

Parking Difficulties

Finding a good parking space is another concern in urban communities. Most times, commuters are stuck in traffic while finding a good space to park their cars. Parking is a problem that needs to be addressed because if commuters don't find where to park, they can't leave the road and meet their appointments or perform other activities.

Public transportation and peak-hours

Buses, trains, and commercial vehicles all serve as a means of public transportation for people In urban communities. Most of the time, these mediums are not enough for the crowd of people available, especially during peak hours. During peak hours, the lengthy queues at stops and crowding at terminals, stairways, and ticket offices are transportation concerns for urban communities.

Long commutes

The distance commuters have to cover from their place of work or business to their homes can pose another transportation concern in urban communities. While urban cities are more commercial with many job opportunities, the cost of living and the exorbitant accommodation price can cause commuters to seek accommodation in more distant but affordable communities, requiring more time on the road.

Solution

While transportation issues can be frustrating, possible solutions can manage some of these concerns. Investing in micro-transit and micro-mobility can be an excellent start to reducing traffic congestion and parking issues in urban communities. A few examples of micro-mobility vehicles are bicycles and electric scooters. Commuters can still get around the city with these forms of transportation. Also, with micro-transit and improved public mass transit, there will be a reduction in the use of private vehicles on the road, reducing the rate of traffic congestion.

LACK OF PREPARATION PROGRAMS FOR YOUTH

By Oyeyemiayo W.

Preparation programs are an excellent way to help develop youth and make them gain insight into their chosen field of interest and passion. These could be in the form of after-school programs, community service activities, scout groups, religious youth groups, and other community-based activities used to create a significant impact on the lives of adolescents. The adolescent stage requires careful guidance and direction from experienced and trustworthy figures. Young people are in a stage where they are curious about almost everything that promises a thrilling experience.

Youths want to create an identity for themselves in the world and secure their self-esteem through any means. Most of them seek career paths and hobbies that they are passionate about, while others delve into specific fields by following the crowd. Hence, there must be preparation programs put in place to guide them. Young people need programs designed to successfully meet their developmental needs and help them grow into productive, happy, and healthy adults.

Unfortunately, many youths do not have the luxury of being guided through adequate preparation programs. Most of them have turned to social media to seek guidance from role models and follow their steps, thereby making wrong decisions capable of destroying their lives in the long run. While social media also has its advantages, community and academic programs promote youth development where young people can meet and learn from influential people one on one, ask life-changing questions, and confide in them. They are the best way to influence young people's lives positively. Can also specific policies, practices, and research can also be put in place to ensure that these preparation programs meet the development needs of young people.

However, the world is changing, and as this change occurs, so are the priorities. There is little agreement on what a youth preparation program should consist of despite many youth organizations, foundations, and initiatives supporting youth development practices and concepts. Preparation programs are diverse and could include non-academic and academic assistance for youths intending to begin their bachelor's or master's degree. For instance, youth can meet weekly under the supervision of an experienced adult to learn about the academic work in the school's curriculum and engage in fun activities like dance performances, leadership development sessions, and calisthenics.

Suppose the activities such as the ones mentioned above are implemented. In that case, there is a possibility that the acceleration of the youth learning process and decision-making abilities would be positively impacted. Thus, there should be intense efforts at both the broader community and individual organizations to support youth development by putting different engaging programs in place.

Conclusively, there need to be more preparation programs made available for youths by school authorities, community leaders, and the government. Adolescence is a delicate stage of development that should not be neglected. At this stage, youths decide what path to take; they decide if they want to impact society or cause havoc and violence. This choice can be influenced hugely by setting up helpful programs that will effectively prepare them to occupy their space in the world.

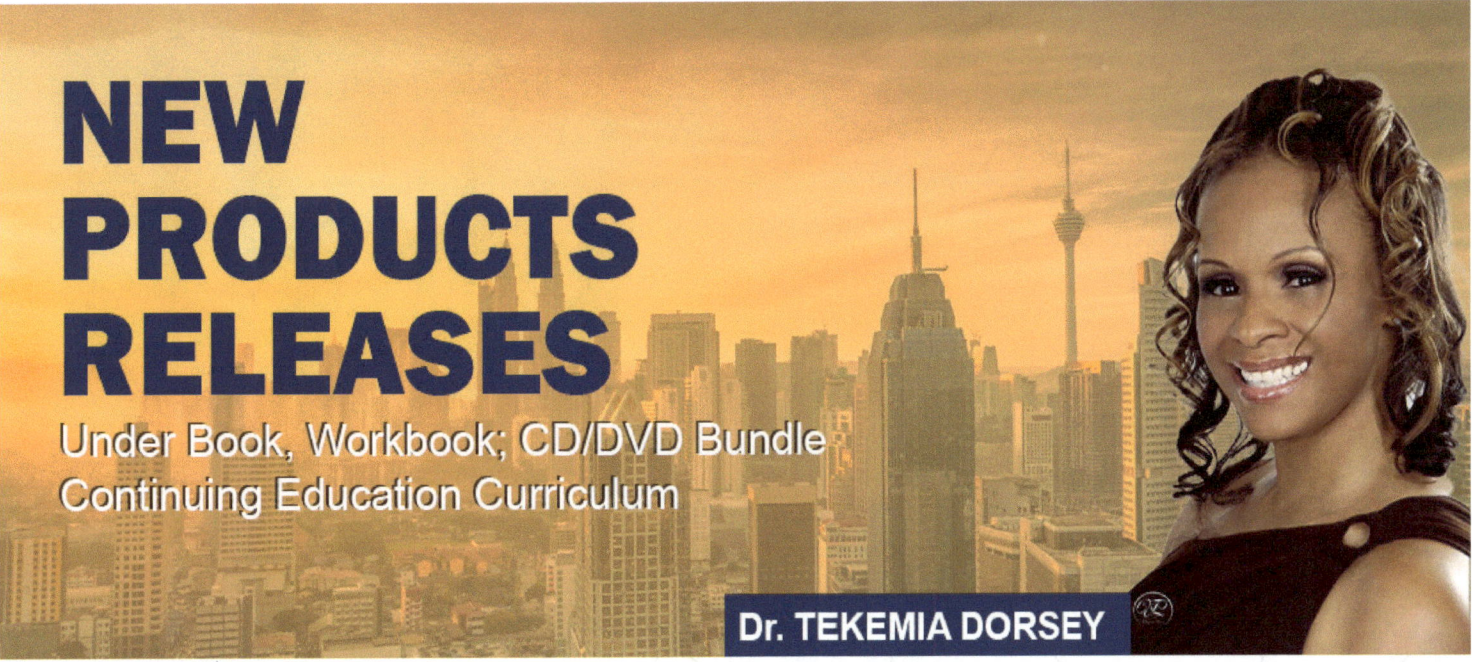

NEW PRODUCTS RELEASES

Under Book, Workbook; CD/DVD Bundle
Continuing Education Curriculum

Dr. TEKEMIA DORSEY

Our Products

 **Build Your Own Blueprint While Becoming A Resource To The Urban Market BOOK**

 **Build Your Own Blueprint While Becoming A Resource To The Urban Market CD/DVD Bundles**

 **Build Your Own Blueprint While Becoming A Resource To The Urban Market WORKBOOK**

 **Build Your Own Blueprint While Becoming A Resource To The Urban Market Single/CD**

Benefits

- Adapted To All Learning Styles
- Self-Paced Program
- Creates A Blueprint That Works For You
- Evokes Action Right Away
- Meets You On Your Level Of Business
- Prepares You For Increase In Funding Opportunities
- Prepares You To Build Community Partnerships
- Prepares You To Expand Your Business Model
- Prepares You To Increase Your Finance & Revenue Streams
- Enacts The Transformational LEADER Within, Plus More

CALL TO ACTION — The First 500 customers will receive a 3 Month Subscription to DTD Urban TV Network.

COUNT ME IN — Receive a 10% Discount if you enroll today DTD's School Of Urban Leadership

www.dtdschoolofurbanleadership.com

Yana Rybak

THE PLIGHT OF EDUCATION IN URBAN DISTRICTS

The quality of education has a significant impact on the future development opportunities of young people and the country.

Unfortunately, there are many prejudices about the quality of education in urban schools that only make matters worse.

Even politicians speak openly about their low quality.

We have recently seen middle- and high-income parents moving to the suburbs searching for quality education.

Financial resources are decreasing. It also affects the districts' demographics and increases the segregation of students.

Even when buying new housing, the main element of choice is the quality of the school, which is nearby.

Segregation.

Most of the students in urban schools are from poor and non-white families. They are also characterized by low-grade achievement and perhaps even poor knowledge of English.

Parents in such families rarely have a good education, so they do not set an example for their children.

Children are often not motivated to learn, read little, or do not want to learn a more complex language. Therefore, children from needy families often achieve lower than their wealthy peers.

Such classes are more likely to be provided by poorly qualified teachers, as their availability is also in question.

In addition, the public care of such schools should be better. They have limited access to technology and lack education professionals.

Students in the suburbs are mainly white children.

They come from wealthy families Usually. They are highly influenced by their parents, who are also likely to have a good higher education. These kids grow up in an atmosphere where the idea of literacy is on a pedestal. They understand the value of school and the skills it can provide.

However, this desire of wealthy parents to take their children to a better environment artificially deepens segregation. Although, research has shown that each child has more opportunities to develop with more diversity in the classroom. Such children grow up more adapted to different living conditions.

Teacher Sorting.

The number and level of teachers` qualifications in the school significantly impact the quality of education.

Teachers may have their preferences in the school area, and the number of pupils in the class. For example, teachers who had previously been brought up in a low-income family were usually not very successful and wanted to work with the same children.

Wages have a particular influence on the choice of employment.

Due to the smaller number of wealthy children in classes in urban schools, wages are naturally higher in the suburbs. It also facilitates the movement of qualified staff.

The number of terrible schools is much lower than expected. Therefore, parents need to get the most true-to-life information about the school to avoid common prejudices. Increasing the number of integrated schools would naturally improve the quality of education in urban schools.

Integrated urban schools are the only hope for quality education for many poor parents.

It should be noted that the poor quality of education in urban schools is only a symptom of the disease of the whole segregated education system.

2nd Annual
ITS TIME TO GO DEEP SUMMIT
September 22 - 24, 2022

CALL FOR PROPOSALS

REACH THE URBAN MARKET TO BUILD COMMUNITIES, LAUNCH GRASSROOTS INITIATIVES AND SCALE YOUR BUSINESS

Dr. Tekemia Dorsey
International Conference Host & Speaker

The mission of the **Its Time To GO DEEP Summit** is to provide business growth and personal development to non profits, small businesses and entrepreneurs while increasing resources to the urban market.

APPLY NOW
www.itstimetogodeepspeaker.com

DOING BUSINESS IN THE URBAN MARKET

(The Need & The Importance)

YANA RYBAK

Congratulations on your desire to start a new business. If you have any doubts about opening it in the city market, it is time to dispel them. There are no doubts.

It is worth reminding starters that marketing involves identifying, understanding customers' needs, and managing resources to meet them.

Understanding the motives of consumer decisions in the urban market helps choose the right strategy for business development.

It should be aimed at improving the image of the city. It will increase the urban market's recognition, value, and competitiveness.

Advantages of the urban market.

In the era of globalization, the right marketing strategy is necessary for development. The most crucial role in the modern economy is given to cities. It concentrates competition for investment, capital, and attention of residents and tourists. Any town is now a different market that has emerged to meet the needs of its target group. Therefore, we cannot overestimate the importance of the urban market.

The urban market is a crucial socialization area, so it is better for young consumers. Identification of their needs will help in business development.

In addition, the urban market is characterized by large free, and underdeveloped commercial spaces. It will be painless to find a place to accommodate, including warehouses located close to highways, which will improve logistics. Well-developed infrastructure will also come in handy.

There are also advantages in labor, as overpopulation affects the cost of human capital. In addition, many want to work in their city.

In addition, by opening up businesses in the urban market, it is possible to take advantage of State support programs for tax relief and microcredit programs.

The urban market is also characterized by accessible technologies, motivated and skilled human resources, and free financial capital.

With all the advantages of the urban market, it is worth considering that the marketing strategy is doomed to failure in the absence of an informed public-private partnership. The assistance of public institutions and private companies is essential to the city's high economic potential. The success of individual private entrepreneurs and legal entities and the city depends on it, as it will cover a much larger segment of consumers. The municipality will support economically poor areas.

What about the weaknesses?

They are also included.

It is risky to start a business wherever it is.

But the urban market adds to the natural economic risks posed by urban agglomeration.
Thus, crime, inadequate land use, restricted land supply due to compaction, defects in urban development, and higher requirements for doing business represent an increased risk.

The urban market is also characterized by frequent changes in the social, political, and economic environment, which will require constant flexibility for the business owner.

And in conclusion.

Urban marketing aims to create a «city brand» and meet the needs of all segments of society. As a result, the application of a marketing strategy should achieve the protection and development of the economic and human potential of the city.

DTD'S URBAN MULTISPORT CONSULTING FIRM
REVITALIZING URBAN COMMUNITIES THROUGH THE MULTISPORT EXPERIENCE

GROW YOUR BUSINESS WITH US

DTD's Urban Multisport Consulting Firm (formerly The Creative GRP, LLC) provides leadership training and business growth development to non-profits, small businesses, entrepreneurs, and youth.

About Us

DTD's Urban Multisport Consulting Firm has been inexistence post 15 years and is the seven-time recipient of the Baltimore Small Business Consulting Award, the 2016 recipient of the USCA Best of Baltimore Training Award and was inducted into The Best of Baltimore Business Hall of Fame.

We Help You

DTD's Urban Multisport Consulting Firm has an accredited online Academy of Workforce Development, Business and Education; a Sports Academy 4 Urban Youth and A DEEP DIVE Academy, in addition to services such as business consulting, program development, instrument creation, operations management, consulting, plus more.

DTD's Urban Multisport Consulting Firm elevates the leader within so that there is less micro-managing taking place in the boardroom, the training center, and the break room. No matter the phase or stage in business, an individual is, DTD's Urban Multisport Consulting Firm We work with individuals just starting out, to those that need business makeovers, and areas in between.

We work in specialty areas such as D.E.I.A Training and Development, Persons with Disabilities Services, Building Communities, Program Development, and getting connected to The Urban Market.

We serve the continental US and abroad; online, hybrid, and in-person. Our staff encompasses over 200 years of knowledge, business, and experience and we want to work with you.

Book a Free Consultation NOW

Core Values

- Innovation Drives Transformation,
- Vision Drive Change,
- Leadership Transform Results, and
- Advocacy Increases Awareness of Needs.

Our Products

Books 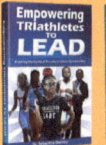   **Workbooks**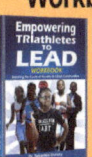

Customization Packages

- Academy of Workforce Development Education & Business (Accredited Online School)
- A Deep Dive Academy
- DTD's Sports Academy 4 Urban Youth
- DTD's Urban Multisport Radio/Podcast Show,
- Plus More

www.urbanmultisportconsulting.com

LEADERSHIP TRAINING AND DEVELOPMENT THROUGH CONTINUOUS EDUCATION OPPORTUNITIES

BY USAMA H.

Many skills are crucial to learn and improve in the digital world, but there is no substitute for Leadership. It is of the utmost importance for any industry and institute to grow and make better progress. In the digital era, everything is changing quickly. It is the era of innovation and creativity. Most industries, whether small or big, require continuous evolution. Continuous positive revolution brings improvement and development to the organization. Organizations are improving their workforce through seminars, coaching, or short courses. The digital era demands perpetual development and innovation. It is pivotal for a leader to continuously learn and upgrade his skills to improve his abilities.

A visionary leader makes improvements to his organization and always performs beyond expectation. Leadership training is of the utmost importance in the digital era. But the question is how to embark on the journey of leadership training and development. An answer to the question is the spirit of learning and the curiosity to explore through continuous education. Leaders have a pivotal role in the success of any organization. Leaders who continuously train themselves and develop their skills consistently achieve their target. They are the people who carry their organization to the next level of success.

The digital era is full of challenges; however, it is the era in which most problem has the fastest solutions available. Before the Internet and modern technology, learning was considered a difficult task. Today one can learn whatever he wants from his comfort zone. Valuable pieces of information and research are accessible to everyone with just a click within a few seconds. The Internet has made learning very easy. It provides a pleasant opportunity for the leaders to foster their learning journey easily.

Leadership training and development demand continuous education, but a leader can't attain a university for the rest of his life for learning. Education plays a crucial role in improving leadership abilities. The most successful founder and entrepreneurs globally have some associations with some of the best educational institutes. Some are graduates of these institutes, and some are dropouts. These leader has never quit learning even after they leave the universities. Research reveals that the top CEOs, managers, and founders of this era read at least 50 books in a year. Bill Gate has said once that he read one book in a week.

Booking reading is not the only source of learning. Webinars, short courses, case studies, Ted Talks, magazines, and research papers are among some of the valuable sources that can help leaders improve their skills and develop their abilities for the better growth of their organization. Online webinars and interviews are good sources to learn about the experiences of founders and leaders. This information will help young leaders and entrepreneurs in their journey. Young leaders can learn from the experiences of other leaders to avoid failure. Leaders are trained through learning from mistakes, continuous learning, and greatly enhancing their abilities.

URBAN YOUTH AND EDUCATION

by Oyeyemiayo W.

Generally, the adolescent year is when youths strive to find themselves and secure their self-esteem. There is usually a strong sense of self during this period for many urban youths who try to carve out a safe space for themselves in the community. Some urban youths find solace in rap music, hip-hop, fashion, and other entertainment industry. However, there are usually some setbacks and challenges in this endeavor, as with every other situation in life. The pursuit of passion and fun cannot and should not take the place of education. While it might be easy to gain acceptance in entertainment with the desired talent, the education sector is entirely different, requiring focus and willingness.

When you hear urban youth, what comes to mind? Perhaps a young person between the ages of 12 and 18 living in an urban environment. Over the years and in some contexts, this term is also a politically correct way to refer to young black people in the news. It also refers explicitly to individuals akin to the "swag" scene or hip-hop community. These individuals often make up small groups comprising of other youths like them and place a sign on their sense of style, their manner of speaking with slang like "finna," "bruh," "nigguh", and "real talk," etc. However, Urban youths come from all areas, shapes, sizes, and colors. Thus, urban youths are not restricted to a specific location or ethnicity.

by Oyeyemiayo W.

Similarly, as Delpit (2006) pointed out, schools are places where young people come to find their places at the tables of power. The stereotype against urban youths, predominantly black urban youth, has become an impediment to getting an education. In recent times, black urban youths have been misunderstood and misrepresented significantly by the media, making it difficult to be taken seriously. Sometimes, their efforts are muted and rejected by schools and the larger society.

However, schools can become places where learning and youth culture intersect in ways that may influence the school success of urban youth if those in authority are willing to acknowledge these youths and extend opportunities for them to partake at the tables of power.

A relationship can exist between school performance and a healthy sense of self among urban youths. The larger communities and schools can help celebrate urban youth culture and their identities that have positive effects by creating a culturally responsive school environment.

Education is a factor of change, a path through which urban youths can reform their minds. The impact of education is strong on society and youths. Education can help urban youths choose and seek their interests. It is sufficient to say that some urban youths have a problematic relationship with education owning to various distractions. Fortunately, there are ways the school and society can help engage young people in ways that they can pursue their passion and still be actively involved in their education.

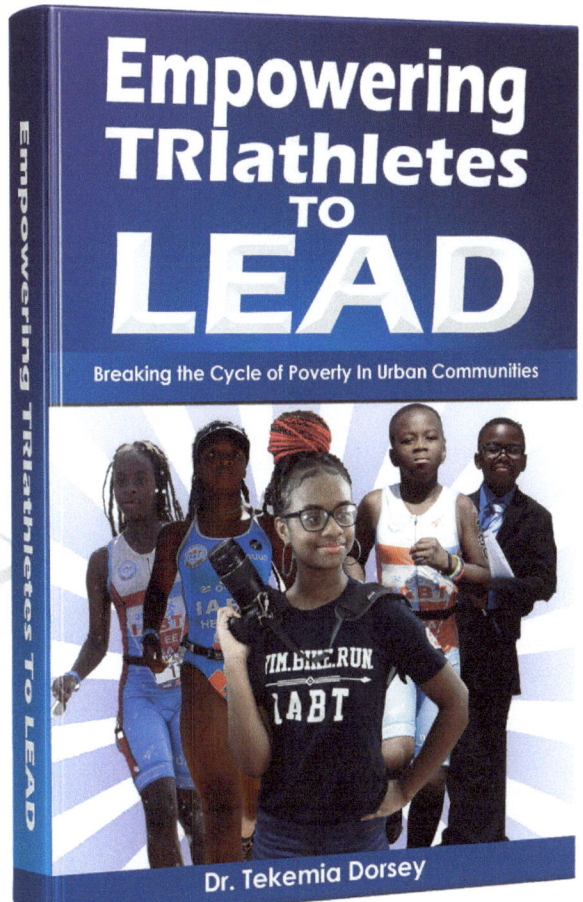
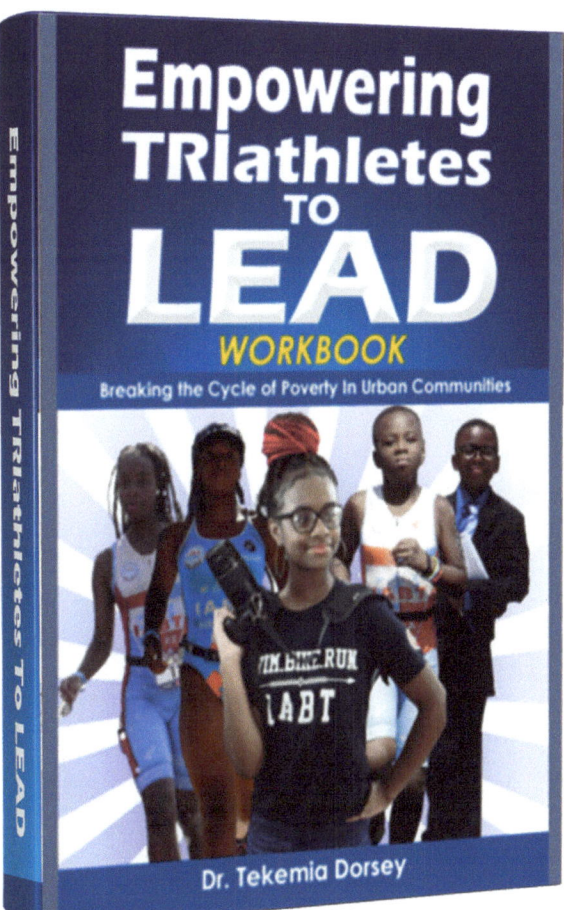

EMPOWERING TRIATHLETES TO LEAD BOOK & WORKBOOK CURRICULUM

Creating a Blueprint to Break The Cycle of Poverty

Designed for Youth Ages 10 -17 years old. A comprehensive, participant friendly curriculum to prepare youth for college and career readiness, workforce development and education, leadership training and development while, decreasing educational disparity & learning to balance health & wealth choices, plus more. Youth create a blueprint that identify current skillsets/interests that lead them to develop a strategic plan to avoid entering the cycle of poverty by the age of 18. A must have to prepare all youth, especially those living in urban communities.

A MUST HAVE TO PREPARE YOUTH TO AVOID ENTERING THE CYCLE OF POVERTY BY THE AGE OF 18.

Available in units of 50 or more

Order TODAY at

www.urbanmultisportconsulting.com

Advocacy

The act of pleading or arguing in favor of something, such as a cause, policy, or interest

Advocacy and Leadership (Urban Youth)

It is the privilege of a democratic, socially-oriented society for everyone to speak out for their own or public interests.

By Yana Rybak

Advocacy.

It is an essential condition for leadership existence and accompanies the last one.
The ability to promote and protect personal and group interests is a characteristic of urban youth that fights for granting new privileges. It is the promoter of social changes, and the engine of urban educational reform. As this is a socially unprotected sector of the population, there is an urgent question of the ability to protect youth rights and legitimate interests.

To achieve its goals, it needs to follow the advocacy cycle, which includes the following steps:

- defining the essence of desired changes
- selection of the strategy to achieve the goal
- action plan definition
- implementation of the plan
- analysis of the results achieved.

It is necessary to possess, among other things, leadership qualities to realize and achieve the goals.

How can we characterize an effective leader?

First, personal development is a priority for him. Small details should not distract him. Only the whole picture is essential. It is crucial to be able to set priorities. The leader's strengths come first, while the weaknesses should be improved.

Secondly, the leader helps in the development of others. He is a good mentor and coach. He shows the ability to manage and drive the group in all undertakings.

Third, he is guided by a pre-defined strategy and applies innovative ideas to act. He is not used to delaying. New ideas do not scare him but force him to adapt, look for advantages, and find a way out. The leader pushes people to manifest unconventional thinking. Decisions must be justified, not rash.

Fourthly, he has a clear civic position. It is impossible to move forward if you do not know the top destination. The leader is introduced to his rights and responsibilities. He is ready to defend his view. Encourages the fight and leads it. He does not tolerate unethical behavior.

There are also several leadership styles, each with its advantages and disadvantages.

- Mentor. His leading role is to delegate. His goal is to develop other people. However, his central ability is to empathize. Every person around him likes that. He is a coach. However, his leadership may not be able to deal with a situation where urgent decisions are needed.
- Idealist. He is inside the idea with the body and soul. He cherishes the idea. You can know him as a motivator. However, it may happen that the belief will consume him, but it will not find a worthy response in the eyes of others. It could destroy established social bonds.
- Achiever. Such a leader is the best among the others and strives for it. He is engaged and stubborn. However, it can play a dirty trick on him. Short of the goal, the achiever painfully experiences failure.
- Innovator. He is creative and strives for changes. His ingenuity inspires new ideas. However, he can become depressed if he has no new ideas.
- A partner is a team player who is ready to support. However, his self-worth is reduced in the absence of a team.
- Advocate. It can be the most substantial style. Such a person can make decisions and take responsibility for them. He is willing to suffer instead of his team and take the fall instead.

The presence of leaders of any type among the urban youth will increase their youth participation in the global network of organizations, councils, and assemblies to protect and promote their civic position.

Join Youth Speakers
On Stage (Fall 2022)

- Evoke Advocacy & Leadership Through Speaking
- No Experience Needed
- 12-Week Speaker Training Sessions
- Better Position Future for Scholarships, Internships, Resume Preparation
- Parent Supported Programming
- Speaking Opportunities for Online and In-Person
- Make A Difference In Your Community, Your Family, and YourSELF

CALL FOR YOUTH SPEAKERS
AGES 9-17 YEARS

APPLY NOW!

Contact NOW for More Details
info@urbanmultisportconsulting.com

INVASION OF UKRAINE BY RUSSIAN TROOPS

A VOICE INSIDE UKRAINE
YANA RYBAK

I believe in the state of Ukraine

I am not a military man, a medic, or a deputy. I am just one of the 12,000,000 people who have been forced to leave their houses in search of safety because of the invasion of Ukraine by Russian troops

I won't avoid the word "war" here because Im 30 years old, and that's what it appears in my head. Another war, thank God, I have not seen

I can't say I was a prominent patriot before the invasion. But I had lived in Ukraine all my life and I liked everything here

I knew that there could be disadvantages in any country, so I did not want to go anywhere. I was the master of my life, and everything worked out for me.

That all changed in 2014.

I did not believe that in the 21st century, one country could occupy part of another country's territory with impunity. We are talking about the Autonomous Republic of Crimea. I thought it was impossible with international norms and all that. And I was shocked. With Russia's financial and military support, someone created two sub-state formations in another part of Ukraine. We understood for what purpose.

That's when the war started, not now.
But on February 24, 2022, the tentacles of this disgusting octopus decided that they could go further.

From that day, all citizens of Ukraine, including me, felt how much they love our Homeland. I became the patriot I had never been before. I have come to adore with all my heart our language, which I had so thoughtlessly used before. I want to see my Homeland prosper. I want a peaceful sky over my head.

No one has the right to claim our sovereignty and independence, our freedom and inviolability.

I cannot live in my house today because I have to worry about my son's safety. I cannot work fully because my office is in Kharkiv, where daily bombs are dropped. I can't speak Russian anymore because I'm ashamed. I can't live because I don't know what I should do next. So I'm just waiting. Life is divided into before and after—two months last like a lifetime.

We thought, at first, it would be over in a few weeks, then a couple of months. Now we're afraid the war will last for years.

They're not going to attack civilian population housing. That's what the optimists thought in the early days. But this myth quickly dissipated with the first civilian casualties. In the first week, a bomb was dropped on a playground in our yard.

Four hundred and eight kindergartens, 623 schools and universities, 206 hospitals, 154 factories and plants, 11 civilian airports, 17 shopping malls, and 91 religious buildings were already destroyed in two months of the war. Are these military buildings? I don't think so.

About 2,000 towns and villages are occupied. Civilians are being killed. Children are being killed. It is the reason I feel hatred and powerlessness. Every day, the numbers increase, and one can only hope that the enemy does not destroy the state's entire infrastructure.

Every day I start and end by reading the news. The patriotism is off the charts. We all want victory so severely. We believe in our armed forces of Ukraine.

The country has watched our government and President turn to other nations for help. It seems logical that Ukraine could not compete with Russia in the number of weapons, missiles, and planes. As we have all realized, the biggest problem was the small number of air defense systems. Because of this, enemy troops were so generous in sprinkling bombs and rockets on peaceful cities.

I think the whole world saw Ukraine's plea to close the sky. It would have saved a lot of people and children.

No one did not believe that Ukraine would be able to fight such a massive enemy with dignity. We should only look at a geographical map to realize that Ukraine posed no threat to Russia. The reasons for the attack are entirely fake and absurd. Russia only wants to grab new lands and revive its empire.

Ukraine has continued to fight for two months now is encouraging and promising. It has caused an increase in military aid from friendly nations.

But the problem remains. All the open sources inside our country, and I'm sure outside our state, are screaming most about the lack of air defense systems. The air defense systems are what we need right now. This need is maintained because Russian missiles are being sent into many cities every day and blowing up buildings.

We do not blame other states for delaying arms deliveries, imposing sanctions, and refusing to limit Russian oil and gas use. We are grateful for all that has already been done for Ukraine. We believe that today the whole world must be more united than ever. Then good will win.

What surprises most about this war is the citizens of Russia. They openly support the war. They demand it like hungry tigers. And it's not just one, two, or ten people but an absolute majority.

I cannot understand how anyone could justify this theater of the absurd. I believe that any reasonable person today with access to the Internet can find all the information to confirm or deny their doubts. All one has to do is search. But it takes a wish to do so. I don't see such passion in Russians.

We are not fraternal nations. We have nothing in common except history, which no longer means anything to them. After all, Russia doesn't realize history. They make the same mistakes someone made 80 years ago. We do not want such brothers. Our blood is different; it has freedom inside.

Ukraine will win. It takes time. It needs help from states that blame war, for which human life is of the highest value.

Ukrainians will never trade their freedom. They won't trade it for anything. And Russia has nothing to offer.

Yana Rybak from Kharkiv, Ukraine.

Congratulations
ITTGD TEEN Writer's Cohort

IT'S TIME TO GO DEEP SUMMIT
AN INTERNATIONAL DEVELOPMENT SUMMIT TRANSFORMING URBAN MARKETS

on becoming
- International Best-Selling Authors
- Achieving #1 Best Seller (Children's Money & Saving Reference) &
- Achieving Best Seller (Education & Teaching) Categories

Beloved Joshua Simons   **Halee Simons**    **Majesty Finley**    **Moriah Finley**    **Philip Wiggins**

Dr. Tekemia Dorsey
Visionary Conference Leader
Editor-In-Chief (The Urban Market Magazine)

TEEN WRITER'S COHORT (FLIER)   SECTION III

SCHOOL SHOULD HAVE MORE FUN

MAJESTY FINLEY

Hi everyone! I am Majesty, and I want to discuss why schools should have more fun! During my eight-year school year, I have worked tremendously hard in school, and I think that should pay off a little sooner with a balance of work and fun. I understand that some may agree, but I think stress levels would minimize if we make sure kids and teachers get to have fun.

So the reason why I chose this topic is that I have noticed that some schools don't balance education and learning with a fun-learning atmosphere. I look around, and it feels more like a work office, to be honest. I have been wondering what if a school would be like a fun playground where you can learn and grow. Also, why not consider having proper playtime and recess for older grades. As I grow older, I enjoy going outside at school, being in nature, and getting fresh air, but I would also love to play! It would be fantastic for older kids to swing, have a place to learn new games worldwide, and enjoy life on break before we go back to the old drawing board. :)

In his article, Why Fun Matters more than you realize, Bryan Harris talks about how schools should be fun for kids. The article says," Why does dopamine matter? It's the chemical most commonly associated with pleasure and reward. When we experience something enjoyable, our brain rewards us with good feelings as if to say, "Hey, that felt good. Remember to do that again." Dopamine makes us feel good, but it also helps with attention, motivation, and memory. Another fact from the article is, "That's an important message: dopamine levels are associated with memory, attention, and motivation! Aren't those the big three (along with getting kids to behave better) that teachers always strive to improve in their students? If students are disengaged and bored, there will be lower dopamine levels. If they are engaged and having fun, dopamine levels increase". Wow!

These facts are Important since it touches my heart about how strict school has become. I see kids like educational zombies rather than living the life of education. Well, the points made in the article talk about how having fun things at school helps you remember stuff and help you behave more which to me would help teachers in their classrooms with students. I think this could help schools because sometimes I hear other kids saying they think the lessons at school are boring. So maybe there could be some school change to be more fun and educational. After reading this, I hope you have some fun, find peace, keep learning and enjoy your life!

Peace - MEF

DTD'S URBAN
MULTISPORT CONSULTING FIRM

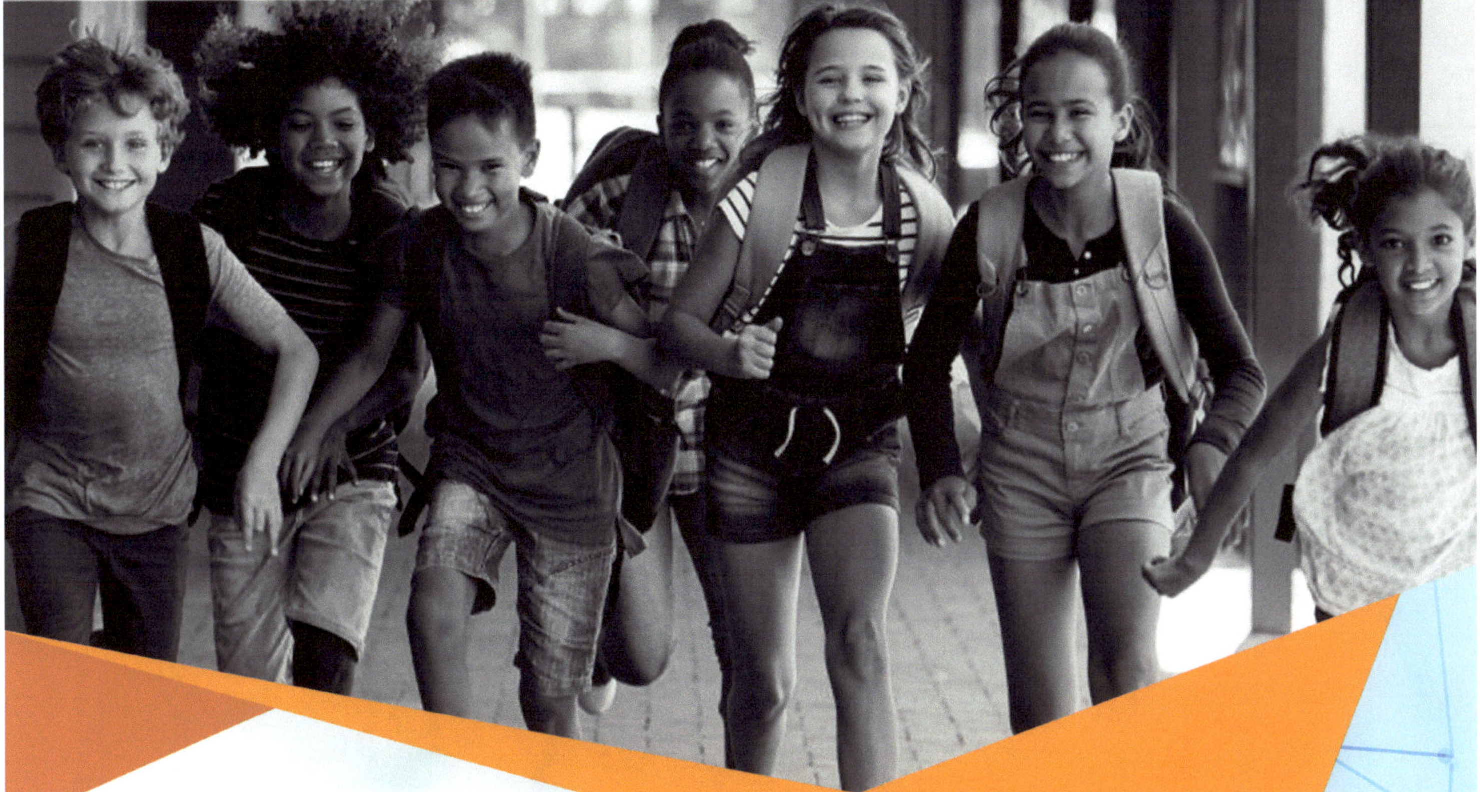

#PROJECT1000

#Project1000 is underway. Our goal is to reach 1000 urban youth in 2022.

We are seeking youth-centered organizations to partner that maybe in need of support services or preparatory programs assistance

Nominate an urban youth or family from an urban community, anywhere in the continental US or abroad that need support services in preparation for life.

To support programming and services - purchase a Tshirt, Mug or combination.

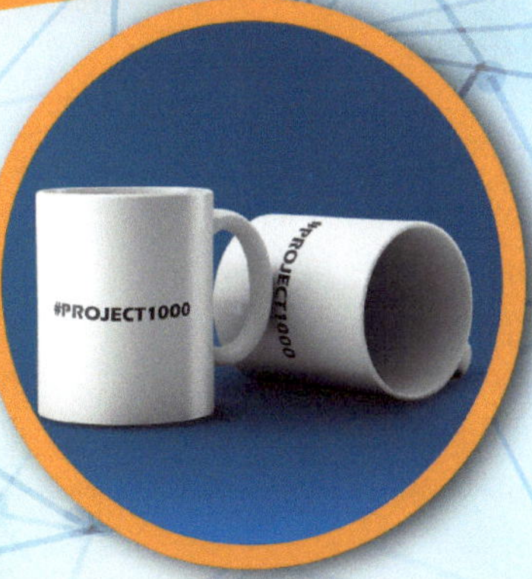

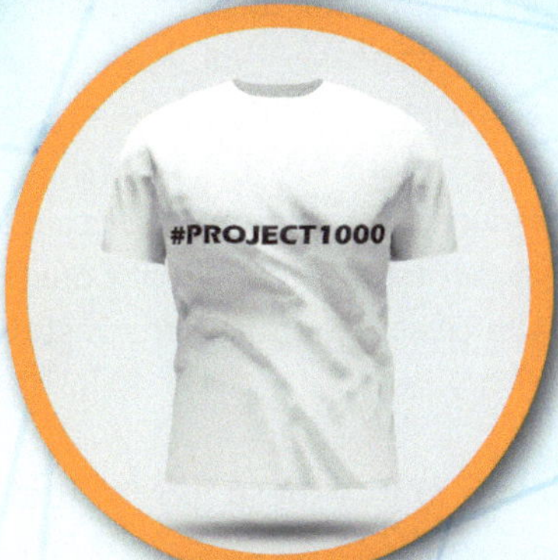

www.urbanmultisportconsulting.com

FINANCES, LEADERSHIP, & EDUCATION

Helping Youth Become Future Leaders

Beloved Joshua Simons

Hello to all the moms out there! My name is Beloved Joshua Simons. I recently turned 14 years old, and I am in the 8th grade. I have a business called Beloved J.'s Public Speaking Firm, where I encourage youth with disabilities to lend their voices for change. I am one of two youth with a business that is part of a local and state chamber of commerce. I am the 2nd Vice President of the NAACP Randallstown Youth Council of Baltimore County. I am also the President of my school's National Junior Honors Society. I've competed in the sport of triathlons for eight years while advocating through this sport on behalf of urban youth worldwide. In this article, I will discuss how you can help your youth become future leaders.

So now, with that out of the way, let's get into the problem that youth face. The problem that youth face is that they aren't getting into the business world and aren't getting any money. They also keep using the phrase "Momma, gimme some," acting like they are at a free for all money lot. This talk will get you a better understanding of how not to have your youth say that.

The main reasons for this are Finances, Leadership, and Education; Finances - youth keep asking for money, aren't spending their money wisely, and aren't putting the effort to work for it. Leadership - They are steady being followers, don't know how to lead, and don't have the right mental state to lead. Education - They aren't focusing in class, significant procrastinators, and want to "fit in" with others.

Let's go deeper into these topics, starting with finances.

Finances: According to a new study by ING Direct, did you know that 87% admit they don't know much about personal finances and, according to renolon.com, around 40 percent have a budget for their finances?

The reasons why your youth they aren't getting into the business world, aren't getting any money, and also keep using the phrase "Momma, gimme some," is because:

- They keep asking for money.
- Aren't spending their money wisely, and
- Aren't putting the effort to work for it.

Even though I use my money as efficiently as possible, meaning getting the stuff that I will know I will use, I have seen my friends experience the exact opposite of what I do. I've seen them spending all their money on gas food (which isn't even that good). Use all their money for things that they won't even look at until they move out (which will also probably throw out), and not be like a civilized person who stops and think about how the thing that they're going to buy is beneficial.

For moms, you can help your youth stop asking for money by making them do chores around the house for allowance. You can help them spend their money wisely by teaching them how to spend it efficiently and as organized as possible. You can help them put in the effort to work for the money by also giving them tasks to complete around the house to get it.

From yflfoundation.org, here are four reasons why financial literacy is essential for youth:

1. It helps them better understand the value of money. When youth understand the value of money, they can handle their finances better. They will be able to know the importance of budgeting, saving, and avoiding unnecessary expenditures.
2. Financial literacy keeps them from being debt enslaved people. If they are financially literate, they will be able to cut your coat according to your cloth. That means they will only borrow that which they can repay.
3. It empowers them on how to invest and create wealth. Being financially literate generally enlightens them in various ways through which we can invest their money and generate more wealth. It can also help you stop spending your money on them.
4. It prevents them from making poor financial decisions. A financially literate person will not easily lure a financially literate person into Ponzi schemes and gambling. This is because they understand the value of money and how difficult it is to earn it.

Having a good sense of money is excellent for your kids if they want to become future business owners.

To all the moms out there. Some of these reasons are as follows:

- They need to know what an account is to input their money into it.
- They need to know how to spend their money as efficiently as possible.
- They need to know how to withdraw/deposit money to save/get their money back.
- They need to learn how to add money to credit cards once they've created one.

When youth see money, they think of spending it as quickly as possible to get what they want versus what they'll need. The thing is, needs are a lot more valuable than wants, and if you teach your kids how to use their intelligent brains to understand better what's a need and what's a want, they will move forward in life.

Leadership: According to forbes.com, did you know that 40 percent of youth aren't motivated to become leaders?

The reasons why your youth they aren't getting into the business world, aren't getting any money, and also keep using the phrase "Momma, gimme some," is because they want to become followers, and they mainly aren't motivated to become leaders.

For moms, you can help them become leaders by being a mentor and teaching them how to become a leader themselves. You can help them stop being followers by showing them the downsides of being a follower and how being a Follower can influence them for the worst. You can help them develop the right mental state to lead by giving them tedious tasks to accomplish and then work up to broader tasks.

According to www.businesswest.co.uk, here are five reasons why leadership is suitable for youth:

1. Implements vision and values

Most businesses have a vision of where they would like to be in the future and how they would like to be perceived by clients, stakeholders, and the wider community. Sometimes both of these can get lost in the day-to-day activities of keeping a business running. Still, a strong leader will ensure staff is reminded of an organization's vision and values and remind them to implement them into their daily actions.

2. Boosts morale

Businesses are nothing without their staff. Constantly recruiting is time-consuming and expensive, so boosting morale to help retain staff is vital to a business's success. A happy, contented workforce who feels appreciated and involved in a company's journey will be more likely to stay loyal to a business while achieving productivity targets – something that a strong leader will ensure—a winning combination for any organization.

3. Ensures effective communication

When big business decisions are made, such as a new strategy or a change in direction, it is crucial to ensure that everyone in the company is informed to reduce the risk of miscommunication. A strong leader will ensure effective communication reaches everyone via emails or staff meetings. Hearing it from the point of authority will diffuse any doubt as to whether the news is trustworthy.

4. Motivates employees

Strong business leaders will motivate employees, whether this is in the monetary form via salaries and bonuses or the implementation of schemes and reward systems that can benefit all staff. They should also recognize hard work and achievement where necessary, so staff feels appreciated for what they do and motivated to continue the excellent work.

5. Provides appropriate resources

Having the right tools to do a job effectively is essential for every staff member, and a strong leader will make sure these are available for the whole organization. Doing this will show that they care about colleagues being able to produce quality work, and they will try to ensure they always can.

For my business, Beloved J.'s Public Speaking Firm, I encourage youth with disabilities to lend their voices for change. I have helped countless youth over these past two years of public speaking to help spread their voices across the globe. I'm great, and all, but the one person who has helped me through all of this is my mother because she has helped me start and create my own business in the first place. She has guided me on the right path to success.

For all the moms out there, having a good sense of leadership is an excellent thing for a future teen entrepreneur because if your youth wants to get their business "out there" in the world, then they would need to know the specific steps that are listed:

- They would need to market their business.
- They would need to be in meetings (which will have them speak).
- They would need to talk to their clients.
- They would need to talk to their employees (because you can't do this alone).
- They would have to step in for others if their peers needed help.

If you haven't noticed, all the things I've just said have been examples of leadership roles that your child would have to take to maintain success.

Education: According to regiscollege.edu, 1.2 million teens drop out of school each year. Also, according to theatlantic.com, 75% of all youth do not like school?

The reasons why your youth they aren't getting into the business world, aren't getting any money, and also keep using the phrase "Momma, gimme some," is because: They aren't focusing in class, significant procrastinators, and want to "fit in" with others.

For moms, you can help your youth focus in their class by having them work with other people/peers to get stuff done quickly. You can help your Youth stop procrastinating by giving your child a shorter deadline than their schools to do their work more quickly. You can help your child not fit in" with others by showing them the disadvantages of what "fitting in" can do to them.

Here are five reasons why education is vital for a future teen entrepreneur:

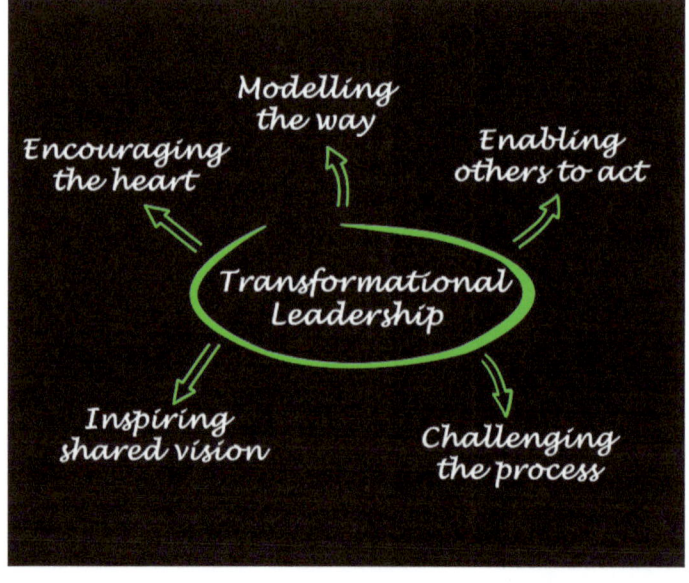

1. Develop Self-Dependency

Education isn't just about learning a collection of facts and knowledge that can't be applied to the real world. Sound educational systems focus on molding future members of society. When a child reaches adulthood, they should be armed with all the tools, characteristics, and knowledge they need to thrive in a world of opportunity.

Independence is a vital attribute for any person. This doesn't just stop at knowing how to cook and get around town. Self-dependency includes learning how to deal with failure, manage certain emotions, and deal with the problematic scenarios that life throws at you.

As they progress down their educational pathway, a teacher's focus on developing these characteristics will grow.

2. Fulfill Dreams and Ambitions

We have goals we want to achieve at each stage of our lives and targets we want to hit. The sense of pride in knowing you've worked to get where you want to be is rewarding and satisfying. Almost always, it requires one vital component - education.

Education provides us with the tools and mental characteristics required to excel in life. Whether your child wishes to be a pilot or scientist when they grow up or aim to open their own business when they hit adulthood, they'll need to use all their academic years to make it possible.

Education unlocks vital skills like good decision-making and interpersonal skills. They will need to draw upon them if they wish to make their dreams and ambitions become a reality.

3. Build confidence

Education and the knowledge about the world provide you provide a massive draw of confidence. A confident child can benefit in many aspects of life. In education, they have the confidence to express themselves or ask for help or clarification if they need it. Confidence is a vital characteristic when working creatively in the arts or a sporting environment.

A more educated child is more confident, which only helps them in their educational pursuits.

Providing they hold onto that confidence into adulthood will continue to serve them well professionally and socially.

4. Make a Fairer World

Education is one of the great levelers. No matter who you are, there is a whole world of knowledge to be absorbed. With it, anyone can grow into whom they want to be and achieve what they want to achieve.

Given everyone the right educational opportunities, they have a fair chance at acquiring new skills which make them employable and competent members of society. Education also benefits other aspects of life like health and wellness, meaning it forms the backbone of a fair society filled with thriving people.

5. Underpin Human Progress

Look around the world, and you'll find the benefits of educating the children surrounding you. From the cars we drive to work, the medicine we help to cure ourselves, and the phones we use to communicate – it's all made possible by education. Our society's emphasis on critical thinking and innovation is realized in everything we touch today.

Beloved Joshua Simons

Just as we are now benefitting from greater transport access, healthier bodies, and improved communication systems, future generations will also benefit from the continued efforts to ensure as many children get the education they need.

As a student experiencing my final years of middle school, I have experienced times when I have gotten unmotivated with schoolwork, and it ended up my grades dropping. This was happening because I wasn't with a group of people who could support me and help me when I needed it. When I finally changed that, everything started going uphill, and I found myself getting better grades, staying organized, and staying on track.

To all the moms out there, education informs people about the variety of essential subjects that will help them later on in life and with a career or gives individuals the skills to interact with others in a community; education also has a variety of widespread effects in communities. Some examples of that would be a decrease in poverty and an increase in health, and it closes the gender gap and provides economic growth.

Now some moms are probably thinking to yourselves: "Why should I have my child become a business owner in the first place, what's the point?" Right? I know you're all out there.

Here are some reasons why they should be, and this is from oecd.org and timeforkids.com: "Youth entrepreneurship is important in addressing high unemployment (approximately twice the adult rate). Young people are more likely to prefer self-employment than adults, but at the same time, their rate of self-employment is much less. "Running a business at a young age can teach you skills that will benefit you in the future.

According to a Gallup survey published in 2017, 40% of kids in grades 5 through 12 plans to one day start a business. Giving it a try early on can help you learn and prepare you for new opportunities.

Becoming a young entrepreneur also teaches you important lessons. These include how to set and meet goals and how to manage money. Finally, running a business teaches problem-solving, critical thinking, and persistence. These skills can help you excel in school."

When I first decided that I wanted to become an entrepreneur, I didn't know what I was doing at that time. I asked myself so many questions that I couldn't control myself from the excitement and nervousness rushing through me. I didn't even know that I was one of two youth with businesses apart from the local and state chamber of commerce. It was exhilarating to watch my business grow.

While I am wrapping this up for nonprofits, consultants, experts, professional leaders, entrepreneurs, parents, and anyone who works with youth from an organization and individual standpoint, consider pivoting your business model to get youth actively involved to become future leaders and business owners. Today, you are cordially invited to become affiliate partners with Beloved J.'s Business Academy, where you will have your affiliate benefits and where we can build collaboration vs. competition for success. Go to www.belovedjspeaks.org and fill out the contact form to get involved.

For those working with youth right now, my goal is to help 100 youth better their lives. What I need you to do right now is to register at least ten youth we know as members of Beloved J.'s Business Academy. The subscription the membership is $20 a year.

Go to www.belovedjspeaks.org to get your youth involved immediately. I hope you enjoyed it and have a great night.

Reach The Urban Market Through

#1 URBAN TV
NETWORK
#1 International Urban TV Network

Contact Arnel, Sales & Outreach Coordinator
sales@urbanmultisportconsulting.com

TEENPRENEURS U.N.I.T.E. TO BUILD YOUR OWN WEALTH

By Philip Wiggins

Hi, my name is Philip Wiggins and today I'm going to share with you how you as a teen can begin to build your own wealth. This doesn't just help you not be dependent on your mom and dad, but you can also build enough money to have lots of fun for your whole life. I want to give you 5 steps that form the word UNITE.

U – Unique Goal. It's important to have a goal that is special for you. It can't be just about making money. You need to be someone who wants to make a difference. Everyone else wants to just make money and doesn't have a unique goal. People are attracted to those who want to make a difference. When I was on TV one time because of my YouTube channel, someone came up to me in the restaurant and gave me $20. He said it was for me because I was making a difference.

N – NOW. What are all the things you can do NOW to make money? What can you do with no help? What could you do with a little help? And what could you do with a lot of help? For the ones that would need help, who would you get the help from, and is it worth it? Or would it be better to do something else you can do by yourself? Is there anything you can do NOW to make some dough? For me, I like making money in the easiest way possible. Something quick and easy with a nice reward. Something I can do anytime I want to, to make some quick money.

I – Individual. you have to be YOU. My mom kept trying to make me a scientist. I'm good at math but it's boring. I never told her though. I didn't want her to get mad. Only when I was honest about what *I* like and what *I* want could she help me make decisions that were about ME and not HER. You have to know who you are and what makes you special because that's the only way to stand out from everyone else trying to make money.

I make bets (like who can I beat at arm wrestling) but when I lived in the dc area my friend had a very popular youtube talking about shoes. Shoes wouldn't have worked for me, so I made money mowing lawns. I'm glad I live where arm wrestles and silly stunts make me money because it's easier and it's fun. But I'm also good at fixing things and painting and lawn work, so I could do those things if I really had to

T – Team get a team. It can be your mom. Or it can be someone you trust at school or work. John Maxwell says leaders aren't successful unless others want them to be. When you get others to love you and want you to succeed they will help you. They will open doors for you and pay you sometimes more than you deserve. My mom says listen to old people they know stuff. She's usually right about this type of thing. I've had my fair share of help in the past 10 years of my life. Make sure you have the right people helping you. Older brothers are always a yes. Younger brothers are always a no. At least my younger brother. He is a controller. Make sure it's someone who loves you and not somebody who will try to control you. Or try to take advantage of you. My little brother won't try to take advantage of me, but he will try to control everything I do so he's not ready to be on my team.

E – Excellence. No matter what you do you have to do it with excellence. You have to figure out what the person who is paying you wants done and then do it just a little bit better than they expect for what they're paying you. That doesn't mean you have to be perfect or waste alllll your time. To be extraordinary doesn't take perfection, it just takes a little extra over the ordinary that everyone else is doing. When you do your job better than expected, you are now the person that people want to work for them, which later on helps your reputation as you keep getting better.

Become An ITTGD Teen Speaker

IT'S TIME TO GO DEEP SUMMIT
AN INTERNATIONAL DEVELOPMENT SUMMIT TRANSFORMING URBAN MARKETS

HALZ S. ENTERPRISES
ELEVATION, INSPIRATION, LEADERSHIP

Requirements:

- Improve Your Speaking Skills
- Learn To Use Your VOICE for Change
- Meet Twice A Quarter
- Be An ITTGD Teen Speaker Ambassador
- Open to Ages 10 - 17 (worldwide)
- Take Advantage of Training Opportunities, plus more!

APPLY NOW
info@halzsenterprises.com

Finances, Education, & College and Career Readiness

Becoming Independent and A Dynamic Leader

Halee Simons

Hello to all the moms out there! My name is Halee Simons. I am 15 years old, a sophomore in high school. I am the CEO of Halz S Enterprises, where I help urban Youth in urban communities become leaders.

I am one of the only two youth business owners with a business part of a local and state chamber of commerce. I am the Youth President of the NAACP Randallstown Youth Council of Baltimore County, MD. I am also a member of NSHSS. I've competed in the sport of triathlons for eight years while advocating through this sport on behalf of urban Youth worldwide. In this article, I provide strategies to assist your youth to become independent and a great leaders.

So now, with that out of the way, let's get into the problem that youth face. The problem that youth face is that they cannot depend on themselves.

The main reasons for this are Finances, Education, and College and Career Readiness;

Finances -
- Kids don't know how to do taxes,
- Kids don't know how to spend $ wisely,
- Kids don't know how to spend $ for their needs instead of their wants

College and Career:
- Youth don't know about scholarships.
- Youth don't know about opportunities that can help them into college for free.
- Kids don't know how to apply for college.

Education -
- Kids aren't getting help in the classroom,
- Kids are too afraid to ask for help,
- Kids aren't being prepared for graduation.

Some solutions to this are as follows:

Finances: 1 in 5 teens lacks an essential foundation for financial literacy.

Having a good sense of money is excellent for your kids if they want to become future business owners

According to a 2015 PISA Study, 22% of teens lack a foundation in basic financial skills. That means they felt they did not have the background to do basic things like building a budget for beginners. So how do we go about making sure all teens have this foundation?

Too often, people look at financial literacy as a concept that needs to be taught in a standalone class. While we love the idea of every child and teen having access to a class like this, we know it's not reality. But what is reality is that many financial literacy concepts can be interwoven into existing classes and coursework. Perhaps an English class allows students to interview other people about different money concepts. A math class encourages students to calculate the actual cost of a credit card purchase by teaching percentages.

For moms, what you can do to help your Youth become more independent in terms of Finances is Budgeting. Budgeting is an essential tool that can help your kids know how much money they have, what to do with it, and what money to spend it on.

From online.maryland.edu, here are four reasons why Budgeting can be essential to Youth:

1. Staying on track for graduation isn't just a matter of good grades and taking suitable classes; students must be able to afford the complete set of credits or classes required each semester and pay for books and other fees.
2. The importance of a budget isn't limited to academics, either. Setting up and sticking to a solid budget can mitigate the amount of debt you accrue in school and help you make the most of your loans, scholarships, or even assistance from family. Taking on some debt to attend school may be unavoidable, but your ability to spend with discipline can help seriously reduce the amount of debt you're left with post-graduation.
3. Budgeting isn't just a college skill. Every student must learn Budgeting isn't just a college skill. Every student must learn budgeting strategies that help them make wise money choices in college and develop financial literacy for the rest of their lives—getting strategies that help them make wise money choices in college and develop financial literacy.

To all the moms out there. Some of these reasons are as follows:

- help them understand the value of the dollar,
- They need to learn how to add money to keep money in savings and add money to a checking account
- Know the difference between a debit and credit card
- how to save for long-term goals, and how to spend responsibly

Teaching children about finances can build financial literacy and give them a more vital ability to manage their finances later.

When Youth see money, they think of spending it as quickly as possible to get what they want versus what they'll need. The thing is, needs are a lot more valuable than wants, and if you teach your kids how to use their money wisely, they can also see how this will benefit them in the long term rather than looking at it in the short term.

Education: According to data from the UNESCO Institute for Statistics (UIS), **about 263 million children, adolescents, and Youth worldwide (or one in every five) are out of school** - a figure that has barely changed over the past five years. The rate of progress, or the lack of it, varies by age group, according to a new UIS paper.

For moms, you can help your youth focus in their class by having them work with other people/peers to get stuff done quickly. Talk to their teacher one on one and list your concerns to the teacher so they can help better adapt to your youth education in a classroom setting. And, also talk to the guidance counselor and principal to help find ways to ease your Youth's minds in getting their task done.

According to https://www.marlborough.org/, here are five reasons why education is essential for a young and inspiring entrepreneur.

PREPARE STUDENTS FOR AN UNCERTAIN FUTURE

Entrepreneurship-focused programs teach students crucial life skills to help them navigate this uncertain future.
1. These skills include problem-solving, teamwork, empathy, and learning to accept failure as a part of the growth process.

LEAVE ROOM FOR CREATIVITY AND COLLABORATION

1. As standardized testing has become more common in public schools, opportunities for students to innovate and collaborate with others have become more scarce.
2. Entrepreneurship education encourages creativity, innovation, and collaboration.
3. These attributes are highly valued by the top colleges globally and will serve your child well beyond middle school and high school.

TEACH PROBLEM IDENTIFICATION

- Students need to learn how to identify problems before solving them.
- Problem-solving has been taught in schools for decades — but the same cannot be said for problem identification.
- Traditionally, problem-solving is taught by presenting students with issues already clearly defined by someone else.
- Problems can only be solved when adequately identified and described in the real world.
- Entrepreneurship education teaches children to identify problems they have never encountered before — a skill that will be very useful in tomorrow's world.

DEVELOP GRIT

1. In her bestselling book "Grit," researcher and professor of psychology at the University of Pennsylvania, Angela Duckworth, states that "grit" may be the single most crucial factor in a person's long-term success.
2. Her research shows that grades, intelligence, and socioeconomic status do not match the characteristic she defines as "grit."
3. According to Duckworth, grit consists of passion and sustained persistence applied toward long-term achievement.
4. The demanding and uncertain entrepreneurship journey requires more passion and persistence than most other activities.
5. This makes an entrepreneurship-focused program ideal for developing grit in your students.

MAKE THE WORLD A BETTER PLACE

1. Entrepreneurs seek to solve problems, meet needs, and ease pain points with the help of their products and services.
2. They are hard-wired to make a difference and make the world better.
3. By participating in entrepreneurship programs, students don't just become ready to create their futures — they become ready to change the world.

College & Career: Results from a multi-year College and Career Readiness survey of 165,000 high school students conducted by YouthTruth, a San Francisco-based nonprofit, found that 45 percent of students feel optimistic about their college and career readiness.

An overwhelming number of students, 87 percent, want to earn a college degree and land a career eventually. But many believe that their schools aren't helping them develop the skills they'll need to succeed after graduation.

For moms, you can help them become ready for college by becoming a teacher/mentor to help guide them into choosing the right college for them. You can enroll your child in a College and Career Readiness Program, which will help them better prepare themselves for success.

According to https://realitychangers.org/ here are three tips on why Youth should prepare for college while in still in high school:

Take college prep classes: Nearly every high school in the United States has a college preparatory program. This academic curriculum is specifically designed to develop the skills and habits necessary for success beyond high school.

Social skills. Communication skills are a bonus in high school, but they're essential in college. Much of your social skill development is a work in progress as you enter college. Still, you can shorten the learning curve by participating in as many school-related activities as possible, academic clubs, sororities & fraternities, and more.

Streamline the process. Tools like the Common Application allow you to apply to multiple colleges with one application. The Common Application not only saves time but it'll help reduce the stress associated with preparing for college.

Now, moms, I know you are probably thinking to yourselves: "Why should I have my child become a business owner in the first place?" "How will they benefit from this? Right? Well, here are some reasons why they should be. According to oecd.org and timeforkids.com: "Youth entrepreneurship is important in addressing high unemployment (approximately twice the adult rate). Young people are more likely to prefer self-employment than adults, but at the same time, their rate of self-employment is much less." Running a business at a young age can teach you skills that will benefit you in the future. According to a Gallup survey published in 2017, 40% of kids in grades 5 through 12 plans to one day start a business. Giving it a try early on can help you learn and prepare you for new opportunities.

Becoming a young entrepreneur also teaches you important lessons. These include how to set and meet goals and how to manage money. Finally, running a business teaches problem-solving, critical thinking, and persistence. These skills can help you excel in school."

If kids can get the right programs to help them know to do taxes, apply for scholarships, and get the right help, they need in a classroom setting. Then, they will be able to better financially and look out for themselves independently and ask less for your help.

For nonprofits, consultants, experts, professional leaders, entrepreneurs, parents, and anyone who works with Youth from an organization and individual standpoint, I want you to consider pivoting your business model to get Youth actively involved to become future leaders and business owners.

Today, you are cordially invited to become affiliate partners with Halz S Business Academy, where you will have your affiliate benefits and where we can build collaboration vs. competition for success.

Go to www.halzsenterprises.org and fill out the contact form to get involved. For those working with Youth right now, my goal is to help 100 youth better their lives. What I need you to do right now is to register at least ten youth you know as members of Halz S Business Academy. The subscription is $20 a year. Go to www.halzsenterprises.org to get your Youth involved immediately.

Its Time To GO DEEP Summit Presents
DTDYouthX Edition
By Visionary Leaders

4X International Youth Speakers
Halee & Beloved Joshua Simons

Dr. Tekemia Dorsey
International Conference Host & Speaker

CALL FOR SPEAKERS

Our mission is to inspire youth and young adults to advocate for change by using their voices concerning issues preventing a positive transformational change in their lives and communities.

Dates: September 22-24, 2022 (International Virtual Conference [Joint Initiative w/Adamas University - School of Education])

September 24, 2022 (In person - Baltimore County, MD)

The Ultimate Hybrid Experience
www.itstimetogodeepspeaker.com

School Protection

By: Moriah Finley

Hi, I am Moriah! School protection is something all kids who go to school need. It is an essential part of school safety and being safe in general.

School protection helps prevent incidents from happening and stops threats from growing. Let's talk about what kind of problems, how kids feel, and how to solve them. One problem is that many kids feel unsafe at school. Some kids who feel this way may be unfocused during the day or have a more challenging time learning in those spaces. One solution is to have security inside and outside of schools.

Another problem is that there are many break-ins in schools. A solution to that is also to have more security and put more cameras in open areas. One more problem that schools face is school vandalism. Others can prevent vandalism, and sometimes it can also be kids in that school. School vandalism can go from writing in books to damaging walls. The solution is to have good ways to keep these things from happening, like, watching around the area.

Even though having more security is an excellent way to start school protection and safety, there are many more ways to help students feel safe. For example, having counselors to make kids feel good about going to school and involving kids in things to help school protection/ safety are strategies to consider for positive change. Altogether, we can stop these problems by taking care of our schools, getting more involved with local schools, and more! By taking care of schools and more security action on the watch, we can stop these problems that kids face at school and help them to feel safe.

THE URBAN MARKET
Magazine

The Triathlon Sport & Urban Youth

Scholar-Triathlete
Halee Simons

Pathways to NCAA Women's Varsity & Collegiate Club Programs

Competing from Elementary to *High School*

NCAA/Collegiate Club COMBINE
Fall 2022 (Baltimore, MD)

$29.99
ISBN 978-1-7355102-7-9

www.ingramcontent.com/pod-product-compliance
Lightning Source LLC
Chambersburg PA
CBHW041548220426
43665CB00003B/66